THE INDIAN MEDICINE MAN

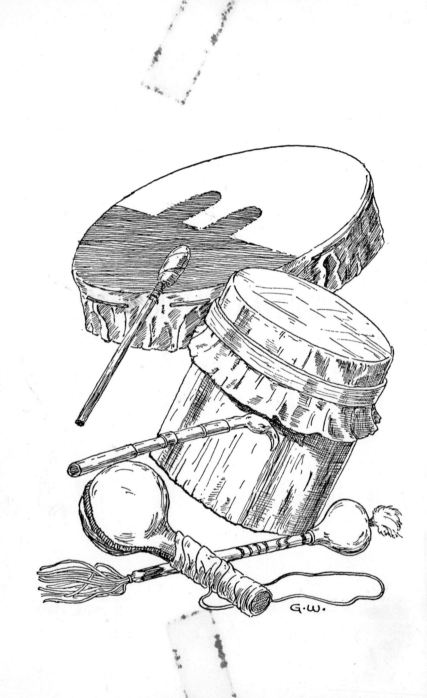

THE INDIAN
MEDICINE MAN

written and illustrated by
ROBERT HOFSINDE (Gray-Wolf)

WILLIAM MORROW & COMPANY   NEW YORK 1966

The author wishes to express his thanks
to the Museum of the American Indian
and its director, Dr. Frederick J. Dockstader,
for permission to quote from
the Museum's publication,
Comments on Certain Iroquois Masks,
by Joseph Keppler.

❖ ❖ ❖ ❖ ❖   ❖ ❖ ❖

CONTENTS ◈

◈ ◈ ◈   ◈ ◈ ◈ ◈ ◈

1 ◆ MEDICINE MEN AND THEIR TRAINING

To the American Indian the wisdom and spiritual powers of the medicine man were as highly respected as bravery in battle, and in some tribes the medicine men ranked socially next to the chiefs and priests.

Some medicine men were healers, others were seers, and some were both. The healers were called upon to cure the sick or to tell what caused an ailment, to remove war arrows from a wounded warrior, and, after firearms were introduced, to take out a musket ball. Those who were seers were able to look into the future and predict what was in store for the tribe or for a hunting or war party.

The Indians believed their medicine men had supernatural powers, which they received from a "dream person"—someone who had appeared to them in a vision or dream. The dream person instructed a medicine man about various matters, and told him what plants and herbs to use for curing different illnesses. The dream person also taught him the medicine songs he used in his healing ceremonies.

The visions through which the medicine man obtained his knowledge were not nightmares. They were dreams he sought through fasting and praying, usually in some lonely spot away from the camp. He prayed not for personal gain, but for dreams through whose powers he would be able to help his people.

A dream person could manifest itself to a man

in various forms. To some it was the sun, appearing as an old man. To others it might be a bird, usually an eagle, or it could be a bear or a wolf. At times the dream person was an old woman or a couple, man and wife. In one instance it appeared as a small worm to a man. Whatever form the dream person took, it always spoke to the dreamer in his own language.

Once in a while the dream person could not help a man fulfill his prayer, and would tell him to go to another place where he would find a person able to do so. Records state that some men fasted for seven days before having a vision, and sometimes they had none at all.

Dreams and visions were of great importance to the Indians. Every Indian went in search of a dream person to guide him through life. A man who had many visions became the great medicine man of his tribe.

Because he was in touch with the supernatural, the medicine man's services were called upon frequently and for many reasons. A good medicine man was wealthy, as his fee was often high. It was paid in horses or buffalo robes. However, if a family was poor the medicine man might settle for less, or other members of the tribe would help pay the fee.

A young man seeking to obtain a medicine dream for the first time usually asked an old medicine man for aid. In so doing, the youth offered the medicine man a filled pipe, telling him of his need.

If he was willing and able to help, the medicine man accepted the pipe. Then, turning to the young man, he painted his forehead, cheeks, arms, and shoulders. If the young man's need was great, the medicine man also painted his chest and back. This paint served two purposes. It made the medicine man's power strong, and the painted designs called the spirits' attention to the fact that a needy man stood before them.

The medicine man then admonished the youth

to be brave all through his vigil. No matter what strange sounds he heard, no matter what he saw, he was to remain where he was and not run away.

His first night alone often frightened the young man, but he stayed on. Should he return too soon he would be ridiculed and scorned by the people of his village. If he was unable to sleep that first night, the young man might remain standing all through the following day. After that, when night came again, he was so tired that sleep came early, and with it, hopefully, a vision.

When food was needed and famine was near, the people asked the medicine man where the hunters should look for game. Then the medicine man began to fast. He painted himself as he had been instructed to do in his dreams, took up his drum or rattle, and sang his medicine songs. At last, looking into his lodge fire, he had a vision. Soon afterward he called the tribal leaders to his lodge and told them how far to travel to find buffalo. Often he told them, too, how large a herd they would find.

On other occasions the medicine man might prevent a horse-raiding party from setting out, because his vision had told him that if they went there would be many widows in the camp. Or his medicine might work to the contrary, showing him that the time was good for a raiding expedition. Then he might even foretell how many horses the men would bring back, as well as the color of the horses.

When someone was ill the medicine man brewed tree bark or plant leaves into a strong tea. He dried herbs and pounded them into fine powders. These medicines, mixed with a little water, were taken orally or put on a wound like a poultice. The medicine man boiled other herbs with animal fat and applied them like salves to wounds, swellings, or sore spots.

The war and hunting charms that tribesmen wore were sung and prayed over, if not made by, a medicine man. He painted dream symbols onto war shields, and blessed and sang over them so they would have the power to ward off enemy arrows.

The medicine man usually wore a distinctive costume consisting of a buffalo robe, worn hair side out, a bear's claw necklace, and a cap of beaver or other animal skin. He also had a medicine bag made from the whole skin of an animal. In it he carried his roots and herbs, his paints and white clay, and other implements and objects used in his cures. Such bags were of great value. They were traditionally handed down from father to son, or were given to a newly initiated medicine man by his instructor.

The ability to commune with dream persons, which required deep concentration, came naturally to some Indians, and they usually became medicine men. A very young boy sometimes had this gift. He would rarely enter into the games played by other children of his age. He preferred to spend his time alone, roaming in secluded places or sitting quietly for hours, observing the nest building of a bird, the activities of the squirrels, or a spider spinning its web.

The boy's behavior was soon noticed by a medicine man. Thereafter, the medicine man would watch the boy, or, as if by accident, join him at one of his lonely retreats. Quietly the older man would sit down near the boy, observing with him the things he found interesting in nature. After a while the medicine man, speaking softly, pointed out some action of the bird or animal they were watching. The youth might affirm that he had noticed this action before and mention other observations he had made.

Though all Indians were trained from early childhood to observe everything around them, this boy soon revealed that it was possible for him to probe more deeply into life and nature around him.

When such a child was discovered, his parents soon were visited by the medicine man. After the proper formalities of greeting the parents, eating the food they offered him, and smoking with the boy's father, the medicine man stated the reason for his call. He offered to take their son with him, to train him as his pupil and helper.

To a boy's parents the invitation was a great honor, through which the entire family gained prestige. It was accepted readily. The boy left his parents' lodge and went to live with the medicine man.

Once the boy was settled in the medicine man's lodge he embarked upon a rigorous period of intensive training, which lasted for years. Day after day the two arose at dawn. After a plunge in the nearby stream they ate a morning meal, then went out together, perhaps to gather roots, bulbous plants, barks, berries, or seeds. Late in the day they returned to the lodge, where the medicine man sorted the day's gatherings. As he did so he

showed the boy how to cut, scrape, boil, and in general prepare the plants they had collected for healing purposes.

The medicine man's dream person gave him the songs to be used in his rituals as well as teaching him cures. These songs he now very painstakingly sang for the boy, making him repeat them over and over again until he could sing them flawlessly. Knowing the songs to perfection was of the greatest importance. If a singer made a single mistake in the wording or in the tempo, the guiding spirits might be offended and cause a patient to die. An offended spirit might also take away from the medicine man the healing powers associated with the song. The songs usually had to be repeated four times; otherwise, it was believed, they would fail to help.

All of the boy's learning served to sharpen his powers of concentration, which in turn helped him to have dreams and visions.

During the long hours of instruction, whenever

the boy's mind and body became tired and unable to absorb any more learning, the medicine man took him to the sweat lodge. After a steam bath and a plunge into the stream the boy felt rested, and his lessons continued.

Learning the many herbs and their uses, together with the proper songs, constituted only a beginning for the future medicine man. Deep meditation, fasting from time to time, and sincere praying to the spirits were also needed.

When the average warrior had a vision, he sought out one of the medicine men to interpret it. He did not tell anyone else about his dream, for it was feared that if he did the dream's medicine would lose its powers. No such loss could occur by going to the medicine man, however, since he had powers of his own. The warrior brought with him a medicine object that was related to his dream experience, and the medicine man sang and prayed over it.

Such a visit became a part of the boy's learning.

Quietly he sat to one side within the lodge while a man described his dream experience, and he listened intently to what the medicine man replied. As the boy grew older and other men came to the lodge, he tried to interpret their dreams in his own mind, before the medicine man gave his thoughts on the matter.

Thus his training continued day after long day. Weeks, months, in fact years passed before the pupil, now grown into young manhood, was finally allowed to assist his teacher. Even when he reached that stage he was only permitted to prepare the herbs, to handle the rattle during a ceremony, or to twirl the bull-roarer, to drive away evil spirits.

When at long last the old teacher felt that he could teach his pupil no more, when he was satisfied with him in every respect, the day came when he told him that he could now work alone—that he could call himself a medicine man.

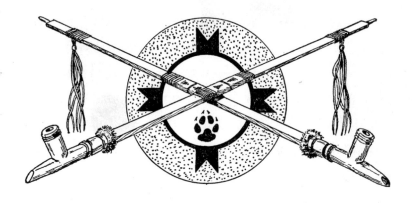

2 ◈   SIOUX MEDICINE LORE

THE Sioux Indians believed that medicine men lived among the Thunders before their mortal birth. During that life they gained full knowledge of what would befall them during their human life on earth, where their work would begin in adulthood upon receiving some sign from the Thunders. If any medicine man disobeyed his sign great trouble would follow him. He might even be killed by the Thunders.

The main functions of the Sioux medicine man were to cure those who became ill and to foretell events, good or bad. He was often called upon to give a newborn boy its first name, too.

The medicine men often used sleight of hand during a healing ceremony, to reassure the patient as well as to impress the onlookers. The patient believed that the evil spirit which had entered his body was now removed and that he would soon be a well man again.

A medicine man performed one such trick by placing a sliver of a charred stick in his mouth, unseen, of course, by anyone. Then, while his assistants chanted and shook their rattles, the medicine man bent over his patient. Sucking for a time on the spot where the pain was located, the medicine man all at once sat up, held aloft the hollow bone tube through which he had been sucking, and at the same time drew the sliver from his mouth. Displaying it for all to see, he announced that here was what had caused the pain. Since it was now out of the man's body he would soon be fully cured.

The Sioux medicine men must have made long preparations for other of their sleight-of-hand tricks, such as carrying burning corn husks in their bare hands. Some men were able to plunge their hand into a kettle of boiling soup and bring out a piece of the meat, without any sign of burn or discomfort.

Visions were of the greatest importance to the Sioux. Any details and rules laid down by the spirit helper in a vision had to be carried out to the letter, lest harm befall the medicine man or his patient. For example, if a man refused to partake of food he was served in another man's lodge, nothing would be said about it, nor would he be urged to eat. It would be taken for granted that the man was under a vow due to a vision.

Many Sioux medicine men were specialists. Some were competent in healing wounds or snake bites, while others cured internal ailments alone.

Not all cures were of the magical type. Massage, bleeding, and herb medicines were used, and sometimes the patient was made to inhale the fumes from certain herbs or roots placed on hot coals. The sweat lodge, so prominent in the Indian's ceremonial life, was also used as a cure for fevers.

If a medicine man had a dream or vision in which the spirit helper was a small animal, such as a fox, an otter, or a weasel, he would obtain the skin of that animal. He then tanned and stuffed it with grass or, more often, with buffalo hair. Thereafter he always carried the skin with him, whenever he went out on sick calls, together with his medicine bundle.

One medicine man, whose dream animal was the otter, was able to cure wounds. Once he was called to cure a warrior who had been shot in the chest with a musket ball. Two of his assistants helped the wounded man down into the river, bringing him out deep enough so that the water

reached to just below his wound. Then the medicine man waded in after him. Placing the stuffed otter skin on the surface of the water, he began to move it back and forth like a swimming otter. Closer and closer he came to his patient, all the while moving the otter skin as if it were alive, until at last the tip of its nose was right in front of the wound.

Then, as if the otter were darting at the wound, the medicine man made four quick passes toward the patient. On the fourth movement the musket ball fell out of the wound.

This sounds like a "tall tale," and, indeed, the medicine man may have used a sleight-of-hand trick. However, the warrior had faith in the healer. Immediately he felt himself cured and walked back to his tepee unaided.

Many of the cures produced by the medicine man may be hard for us to comprehend, but the physical life the Indian lived in the open was very different from ours. He did not overburden himself with too much clothing, and his daily life was spent hunting or on the war trail. Perhaps his activities and his way of life enabled him to heal faster and more readily than is possible for a man today.

The Sioux medicine man also had a fair knowledge of human anatomy, and he was able to set broken bones. After setting a bone he took a large piece of rawhide that had been soaked in water until it was very soft. He wrapped it around the broken bone, holding it in place with bands of more soft rawhide. As the rawhide dried it shrank, molding itself to the arm or leg. When it was dry it made a cast very similar to the plaster cast used by doctors of today.

The medicine man took care of sprains or pulled muscles, too, and in time he learned to sew up deep wounds. His thread was a fine strand of sinew, and his needle was made out of a thin sliver of bone.

The dress of the medicine man varied with his

work. When carrying out a ceremony, he often dressed in an elaborate costume. A whole bearskin reaching from head to heels all but covered him, while the skins of smaller animals and birds hung from the bearskin.

Another of his costumes was one of the finest to be seen within the tribe. It consisted of a soft tanned elk skin with long, slender fringes, embroidered with quill or beadwork bands on the shirt and leggings. A horned bonnet or a turban of wolfskin topped the regalia.

The medicine man's powerful medicine bag, or medicine bundle, was rarely sold. He usually passed it on to his son, or possibly to one of his best pupils.

Special societies within the tribe had their own medicine bundle, too, as did the tribe itself. Each bundle was cared for by one member of the tribe or the society. To be such a keeper was an honor that gave a man and his family great prestige. The

caretaker of a bundle had the right to decorate his tepee with painted designs. Often he painted the buffalo, the otter, the elk, or whichever animal had been the dream animal of the medicine man when the bundle was first given to the people.

It was costly to be the keeper of a society's bundle. Whenever the bundle was opened in public, the keeper had to give a feast for all who participated. He provided the costumes for the occasion as well. In many cases a special horse, never used for any other purpose, was required to carry the bundle during ceremonies. This horse was in charge of the keeper too.

Because of the expense involved, a keeper might in time wish to let the responsibility go to someone else. After he let it be known that he wanted to transfer the bundle, a great warrior would come forth to take it over. The transfer was made with much ceremony, lasting often for several days, and it was always a great expense to the new owner.

The large tribal bundles, such as the Beaver Bundle and the Medicine Pipe Bundle, were a little harder to transfer, for they required even more costly, elaborate ceremonies when they were opened. Many more people attended, so more food was needed, and gifts were given to those who helped with the ceremony. These helpers were many.

The keeper of a tribal bundle announced that he desired to have someone else take over the bundle. If no one made the gesture to accept, then the caretaker of the bundle could sneak into another man's tepee during the night. There, with a few of his friends, he awakened the man by touching him with the pipe stem from the bundle. When a man had been touched in this manner he dared not refuse the bundle, for fear that ill would befall him and his family.

A warrior whose personal medicine bundle had shown its worth might wish to sell it at high cost. This man, too, because he owned a valuable bundle, was permitted to paint his tepee with special designs. Usually he depicted his most outstanding war exploits.

3 ◈ IROQUOIS MASK MEDICINE

THE Iroquois called themselves *ongwe onweh*, the real men, for they were created by the Great Maker of All. Among other things, the Great Maker gave them control over the life and death of all living things except themselves.

The first of the real men was, according to the old storytellers, the only man among the earth's creatures. In time he became boastful and self-satisfied. He told the deer that although it could run faster than he could, he could make a bow and arrow with which to kill it. He bragged to the bear in the same manner. He came to think of himself as the ruler of all, until at last he thought himself greater than the Great Maker.

Finally the Great Maker had had enough. The next time the lone Indian boasted before the animals, the Great Maker came out of the forest and stood before him. To the man he was a total stranger, and during their conversation the Indian could not refrain from boasting about his great powers. At last he boasted that he could even move the mountains.

On that the Great Maker challenged him, and they went out to a flat piece of land from which they could see a distant mountain. Standing side by side with their back to the mountain, the Great Maker told the Indian to prove his boast, whereupon the Indian commanded the mountain to move close to them.

For several moments they stood in silence, and

then they turned around, only to find the mountain standing exactly where it had always stood.

Now it was the stranger's turn. He, too, commanded the mountain to move, and after a few moments he told the Indian to look behind him. The Indian was very angry over his failure, and in his anger he turned around quickly. The mountain was now directly behind them, and when the Indian turned he slammed his face against an outcropping ledge. So great was the impact that his whole face was distorted. His lips swelled up, his nose became crooked, and he lost most of his voice, so that he could only utter a timid, "Han-han."

The Great Maker then told him that from now on more people would come to live on earth. When they appeared Crooked Face would have the task of protecting them against all causes of ill health.

As the Great Maker had foretold more people did come, and Crooked Face became known to them as "the Helper." He also received the honored title, "Our Grandfather." He instructed the people in conducting medicine ceremonies to overcome sickness, and he carved a false face for them in the image of his own distorted features.

Crooked Face's instructions began to spread among the people and the power of the mask grew. Other masks followed the original, and in time the Iroquois formed the still-existing False-face Society.

Contrary to the custom of most other tribes, the appointed leader of the False-face Society was a woman, a person of outstanding character. To the Iroquois she represented Mother Earth, the soil. Her badge of office, which she carried during public ceremonies, was a staff. It was decorated with a miniature false face, a small corn-husk mask, and a miniature turtle-shell rattle, which symbolized long life.

A mask had to be carved from a living tree, for it was believed that this gave the mask life. The basswood tree is soft and its fiber is absorbent, so

it was most often used. Once the tree had been selected sacred tobacco was burned before it, and one of the oldest medicine men rubbed its bark with a turtle-shell rattle, reverently asking the tree to continue its life spirit and share it with the mask to be carved from it.

The mask was then roughly outlined in a preliminary carving. Next it was split away from the tree trunk, and the "wound in the body" of the tree was offered incense from the sacred tobacco. Thereafter, the rough-hewn mask was taken to the home of the carver, where he finished, painted, and decorated it in the proper manner. The new false face was then inducted into the Society, an occasion that demanded the greatest of ceremonies.

All the false faces were carved to represent terrifying characters, in order to frighten away the evil spirits that brought a patient's sickness. Some masks were red and carved with a deeply ridged forehead, which gave them a worried look. They

were supposed to possess great medicine powers.

While a person was wearing a certain false face he took on its power and its identity, and he was referred to by the name of the mask. One of the red masks with a ridged forehead was the Doctor, or Medicine Mask. It not only possessed the power to drive out disease, it was highly important in rituals other than curative ones.

During public ceremonies of the False-face Society the Doctor called upon each member to dance as a devotional obligation. When the New Year's ceremonies were held, it was the duty of the Doctor, or at times the Doorkeeper, another powerful mask, to stir the embers and ashes of the old fire. Those ashes were then distributed to the four inner and four outer corners of the lodge. Then a new fire was made and blessed by those masks.

This New Year ceremony should not be confused with the one celebrated in our society January first, as the Iroquois New Year came during late January or early February. At that time the masks told the people to forget the past year's disappointments and troubles. They advised them to forgive their personal enemies, and to wish all the people a year of health, happiness, and well-being for their entire household.

Medicinal plants were of much less importance among the Iroquois medicine societies than was strong magic. Medicine was to them the mysterious quality of spiritual power, found usually by calling upon the supernatural.

When illness befell a person, the False-face procession entered the dwelling of the sick man. There the medicine men formed a circle and hung a number of robes or blankets around the patient. They burned sacred tobacco, like incense, in the sickroom. To drive out the evil spirits and the pain they caused, the medicine men took handfuls of live embers and hot ashes from the hearth. Some of these they blew upon the patient with outspread lips, "those upon which evil cannot rest," and they rubbed the remainder on the area of the body that was afflicted. During this ceremony the Corn-husk mask guarded the doorway.

In the earliest days the Iroquois surrounded their medicine societies with great secrecy. But in the eighteenth century, after the Iroquois had been defeated, they felt hopeless and frustrated, and in 1799 a prophet named Handsome Lake came to teach them new ways. Handsome Lake had a vision. He added new ceremonies to the old, he forbade secret meetings of the medicine societies, and he helped the Iroquois to survive and to fight the plague of alcohol. He gave their religion a form which survives today.

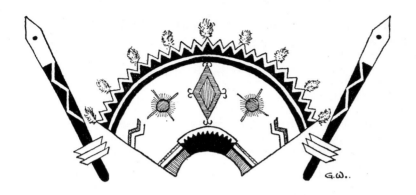

4◆ APACHE MEDICINE MEN

THE Apache medicine men, like those of several other tribes, were sleight-of-hand artists. One of them was noted among his people for a great feat he was able to do. By merely holding his hands up toward the sun, he could light his pipe.

As this was back in the 1880's, the answer could very well be that, unknown to his fellow tribesmen, the medicine man had obtained a small magnifying glass, either at the trading post or from a soldier, and had learned its use. In fact, magnifying glasses were then known as burning glasses.

However, tricks could not always serve the medicine man, and many of them did have great powers of concentration. Records show that one medicine man was able to tell a person where to look for something that had been stolen from him. After being told what was missing, the medicine man prayed for a long while, then went into a deep sleep. Upon awakening he could tell his client not only where to look for the stolen item, but who had stolen it from him as well.

The medicine men controlled all preparations for a war party, and on the trail of an enemy their power was undisputed. If it was at all possible the medicine man took a nightly sweat bath on the war trail, and there he sang and made medicine for the good of the party.

When sickness struck the medicine men took charge. Two usually cared for a case, and they called upon friends and relatives of their patient to supply wood for the fire, help with the singing, and perform other chores.

The only musical instrument they used while singing over a patient was the drum. If the patient was very ill, the medicine men built a great fire close to him and danced around it.

During the medicine men's singing the patient's friends helped sing the refrain, though they could not understand the words. The medicine men often relied on mysterious syllables somewhat like a magician's *hokus-pokus* or *abracadabra*. However, the monotonous singing had a beneficial effect upon the patient. It undoubtedly tended to lull him into sleep, deep and sound, from which he often awoke refreshed and much improved.

If the medicine man felt that the illness was caused by an evil spirit that had entered the patient, the treatment became quite different. He then called in two or three other medicine men to help. Seating themselves around the patient, they beat loudly on their drums, sang and shouted, and in general made as much noise as they could in the hope that it would frighten the spirit away.

When ceremonial feasts and dances were held, the medicine men took charge. The Mountain Spirit Dance was a dance that was performed only on the most solemn occasions, and several medicine men worked together during the ritual.

The eldest medicine man was the drummer as well as the leader of the ceremony. He wore no paint or decorations of any kind. Three other medicine men, however, made up for his lack of show. Their upper bodies were covered with a greenish-brown paint. On each arm was painted a yellow snake, its head toward their shoulder blade. One man wore a two-headed snake, which had one head at each end of its body.

These helpers also wore insignias painted in yellow on their chest and back. To make sure that these symbols would be powerful, the leading medicine man had drummed and chanted medi-

cine songs while the symbols were being painted on. One medicine man had a yellow bear on his chest and a spirit symbol on his back. The second also had the bear totem on his chest, but he wore a zigzag for lightning on his back. The third had the lightning symbols front and back. All wore buckskin kilts and the high-topped moccasins of the tribe.

The three assistants also wore masks made from black-dyed buckskin. Shaped roughly like a sack, the mask fitted over and completely covered their head. They were held in place with a buckskin band dyed red, knotted around the wearer's neck. Symbols were painted on the masks, too, and three holes were cut in front—two for the men's eyes and one for them to breathe through.

Extending from the top of the masks was a most unusual headpiece. It was made from strips of the Spanish bayonet, a desert plant, and was painted in symbolic colors of yellow, red, and blue. Yellow represented the sun and the moon; red represented life; and blue stood for the sky. The place where the headpiece was fastened to the mask was covered with feathers—eagle feathers to please that powerful bird, turkey feathers as an appeal to the mountain spirits, and white gull feathers for the spirits of the waters.

Each of the three assistants also held two sword-like wands, made of thin strips of wood and ornamented with snake lightning painted in blue.

During the ceremony the medicine men made a peculiar whistling sound while bending to the left and to the right, forward and backward. Each time they bent until their head was level with their waist. Then quickly they spun around in a full circle, first on the left foot, then on the right. Next they made cutting and stabbing motions with their swordlike wands, to drive away evil spirits.

One woman among the spectators carried a sick baby in its cradleboard. Toward her the three medicine men now turned, walking slowly. As they came before her, she knelt and held the cradleboard up to them. The medicine men struck at and around the cradle with their wooden weapons while the mother turned the cradle so that the child faced each of the four winds in succession.

At last one of the medicine men took the cradle with both hands and pressed it to his chest. Then he lifted it to the sky, held it toward the earth, and finally again turned it to the four winds. All during this performance he pranced, whistled, and snorted while the mother and her woman friends made piercing shrieks.

One by one the other medicine men took the cradle and carried out the movements made by the first. That ended the baby's part in the ceremony.

The medicine men, however, continued their swinging, bending, and spinning to make their medicine strong and powerful. The dance had to be continued as long as there was any fuel left to be added to the fire. Should they stop before the

large pile of wood was used up, the ceremony would surely bring bad luck.

The ceremony lasted four nights, and the colors and symbols painted on the dancers' bodies varied from night to night.

Many Apache medicine men had a good knowledge of the curative qualities of herbs and plants, yet they preferred their songs to medication.

The pollen from one plant, however, was of immense importance to all Apache, men as well as women. From their belt or sash, or suspended on a cord around their neck, hung a small buckskin bag. Some bags were plain, others were ornamented, but each contained a yellow powder that looked a good deal like fine cornmeal. It was the pollen of the tule, a species of the cattail rush that is found growing in small ponds throughout the Southwest.

So important was this pollen to the Apache that even the tiniest baby had a bag of it. Either he wore it as a necklace, or it was fastened to his cradleboard.

An Apache's first act upon getting up in the morning was to blow a pinch of this pollen, called *hoddentin,* to the sun. The Apache also offered pollen to the moon, especially the crescent moon, to the morning star, and to some of the animals, the greatest of which was the bear. The puma, or mountain lion, the snake, and the eagle were also important animals.

When he was tired from walking long and far, the Apache placed a pinch of *hoddentin* on his tongue to restore himself. No warrior would think of going on the war path without a small pouch of the yellow powder at his belt. If a warrior was hurt, wounded, or taken ill on the war trail, the medicine man with the party walked in front of the horse or mule upon which the warrior rode. As he walked, he scattered small pinches of *hoddentin* on the ground, so that the patient's path would be made smooth.

When returning from war the Apache held a dance. On the morning of that day they threw a pinch of powder to the sunrise and to the four winds.

After corn was planted the medicine man buried eagle plume sticks in the field, scattered tule pollen, and sang over the field. When the corn was partially grown the medicine man again sprinkled pollen over it.

As a medicine the yellow powder was indispensable. The medicine man applied it to the forehead of a sick man. Then he sprinkled it in the sign of the cross on the patient's chest, and if the man was especially ill the medicine man also made the sign of the cross with *hoddentin* on his head, breast, arms, and legs. The pollen was sprinkled around the patient's couch, and pinches of it were put on the forehead of the chanters. Lastly, the medicine man placed some *hoddentin* on his own forehead and put a pinch of it on his tongue.

The sign of the cross was used often among the

Apache, and they made crosses from wood as well. It did not have a Christian meaning for them, but represented the four cardinal points. A warrior painted it on his moccasins to keep him from taking the wrong trail in strange country.

The pollen of the tule must have been with the Apache for a long, long time, for one of their legends says that the Great Spirit spilled it across the surface of the sky, thus creating the Milky Way.

5 ◆   NAVAHO MEDICINE RITUALS

THE Navaho medicine man, who was highly honored, worked with his people in many ways. Experiences such as the following would not have been uncommon for him.

The medicine man stepped through the hogan door, turned, and carefully let the blanket close the doorway. Silently he mounted his horse and rode off.

The young man over whom he had prayed, to whom he had offered the magic of the Old Medicines, had died.

After he had left, the relatives of the dead youth would come and bury the body within the hogan. The upper logs of the hogan would be torn down, and no Navaho would ever thereafter go near the place.

The medicine man now rode past several hogans. In some of them were people who were ill, but he avoided them all. For the next seven days, the medicine man made it a point to avoid meeting anyone. He did not return to his own hogan, but camped within the maze of canyons through which he rode. Day after day his keen eyes searched for medicine herbs, and by the end of his lonely trip he had a large collection of herbs, seeds, and grasses.

On the evening of his seventh day he rode to the top of one of the canyon walls. The sun was going down as he dismounted. In the glow of the sunset he knelt, and with head bent he prayed to the Faraway Gods, and to the Fathers of all Medicine Men, the Ancient Ones. Finally, in the last dim rays of the sun, he rose to face the east, the north, the west, and the south.

The next day he returned home. Near his hogan he made a fire from wood of the piñon pine, and by its light he fashioned a medicine mound of earth, into which he placed all the new medicines from the canyon. After rounding off the top of the mound he placed prayer sticks on it. This structure was his medicine prayer, and he slept next to it all night.

During the five days that followed he fasted and did not sleep. His mind and thoughts were on the ills of the world. He thought of the past, of the present, and of the future. All the while he willed his medicine to be strong as he himself grew stronger in his thoughts. Again and again he prayed to the Ancient Ones, asking for their assistance.

When the sun went down at the end of his last day of fasting and praying, he finally lay down on a sheepskin by the mound and, pulling his blanket close around him, he slept.

When the first warmth of the sun touched his face the following morning he sat up. Then he removed his medicine from the mound and brought the articles into his hogan. Awaiting his return, his wife had prepared a meal for him, and after eating he rested.

A few days later a messenger summoned him to a hogan to attend a patient. The messenger told him what the patient could pay and gave him directions to the hogan. After accepting the call, the medicine man set a date for his arrival, about four days later. The patient's family needed this time to make everything ready.

When the medicine man arrived at the sick man's hogan, he dismounted and took his medicine bag from his saddle. Inside the hogan he found his patient resting on a sheepskin and some blankets. Greeting him, the medicine man seated himself near the patient's head. For several minutes he sat in silence. Then he started a chant, one of the old, old songs. His voice was so low that only the sick man could hear the words.

The chant went on and on, and as it continued the fear and pain on the sick man's face gradually changed to a look of peace. Then he closed his eyes.

The chant faded on the lips of the medicine man, and as it did he gently placed his hands on his patient's forehead. After a while he removed them and, reaching for his medicine bag, he brought forth a small buckskin bag containing a yellow powder. He mixed a small amount of the powder in a shallow dish with a little water. When it had become a thin paste he again turned to the patient. Gently but firmly he began to spread the paste over the patient's face, avoiding only the eyes and the mouth.

This done, the medicine man once more placed

his hands on the patient's brow, saying, "Think nothing now, and close your eyes." Chanting these words again and again, he kept kneading the sick man's forehead.

An hour passed and the chant went on. Now the medicine man's fingers slowly moved from the patient's brow and down over his face. At last, when the medicine man removed his hands, the paste had dissolved completely and the patient was sound asleep.

Important medicine ceremonies lasted from five to nine nights, and a special large hogan was constructed for them. The powerful and mysterious Mountain Chant was a nine-night ceremony. Its purpose was to heal sick persons and to bring all who participated into a closer contact with the *Yeis*, the gods of the Navahos' inner being.

The medicine man in charge had great prestige. His responsibility was also great, and he selected his assistants with much care. Often these helpers were the young men who were living with him as his pupils. The helpers made prayer sticks and prepared the many important herbs to be used. They also performed the ritual of purifying the hogan.

In front of the hogan, placed on white sand, were many small sacred objects, to ward off evil spirits and to protect the medicine men who were working inside, preparing for the night's ritual.

On the first day of the long ceremony, the patient's hair had to be washed in yucca suds. He had been through the ceremonial sweat bath, and he had been made clean within through the use of special emetics. Finally he was blessed with sacred pollen and was now ready to be noticed by the *Yeis.*

The medicine man's work, however, was just starting, for although these ceremonies were called night chants, much of the work took place in the daytime.

For a ceremony the size of the Mountain Chant

the medicine man usually made four large sand paintings, which required many bowls of colored sands and pigments, inside the medicine hogan. The sacred colors were prepared with fine grinding stones. Under the guidance of the medicine man, his assistants dribbled the colors from between their thumb and index finger. Offerings were added to the painting—turquoise, seashells, small bits of cannel coal, and feathers.

Sometimes for a private healing ceremony the medicine man made a small sand painting on the floor of the patient's hogan. Navaho legend says that the figures depicted in the sand paintings were first drawn on the clouds by the War Eagle God. He taught the Indians to make the figures with colored ground sand, or sand from the Painted Desert. The War Eagle God knew that sand paintings could not be stolen by an enemy. He cautioned that the paintings must be started at dawn and destroyed by sundown, lest evil spirits use them.

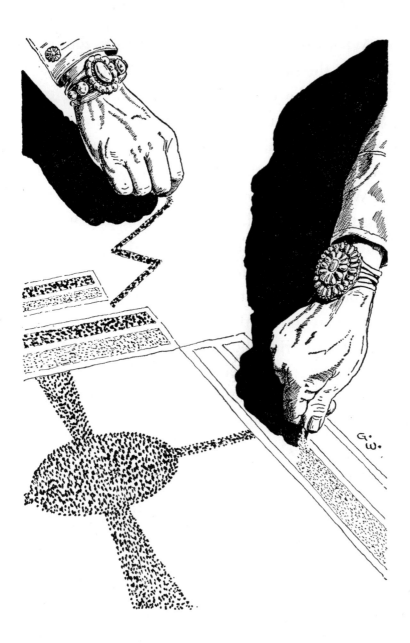

When the sand painting was ready, the offerings in the sand were removed. The patient was seated in the center of the design, facing east. Smoke curled upward through the smoke hole. Around the walls sat the assembled Indians, but of this audience the patient seemed unaware.

With intense concentration the medicine man led the singing, while one of his helpers wet the soles of the patient's bare feet and transferred to them a small amount of sand from the painting. While the low chant continued the helper touched other parts of the patient's body and limbs, each time transferring the proper portion of the painting to the spot he had touched. The purpose of this ritual was to transfer the powers of the gods who dwelled in the sand painting directly to the sick person. The transfer always began at the feet, as was the way of the gods. Working upward, the evil was finally driven out through the mouth. Good would then be established again, and harmony of mind would restore health.

As the medicine man's assistant worked, he rested from time to time, holding his hands suspended in midair. The chant, however, continued. Hour after hour it rose and fell hypnotically. It filled the hogan with a strange, mystic rhythm that reached into every nook and cranny of the building.

At last, the medicine man gave a signal and the chant stopped. One of the helpers lit a sweet-smelling incense, and while the patient was made ready to leave the hogan the medicine man intoned another chant. It had a different tonal inflection as he sang for the patient's health, restoration, and identification with the *Yeis*.

By now it was late afternoon, and the sand paint was destroyed fully. The sands were scooped together in a large heap and transferred to a blanket. The assistants carried it away and disposed of it in a special place.

After sunset the patient—or patients, for there were often more than one—had a place of honor

at the dancing that further invoked the approval
and blessings of the *Yeis*.

As the result of such a chant, the Navahos'
spirits were renewed and their lives rededicated,
and they were assured of new hope.

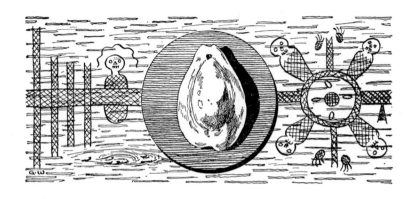

6 ◆ THE OJIBWA MEDICINE LODGE

THE man of the Ojibwa family did the hunting, fishing, and trapping. The woman had charge of the many household duties. Thus the success of the entire family depended fully on good health.

The older people of the tribe had a knowledge of herbs which was useful for healing cuts and curing lesser ailments. This knowledge was important especially during the months when a family lived alone, away from the rest of the tribal members, as was often the case.

The Grand Medicine Society, the Midewiwin, was formed to safeguard and prolong human life, through the knowledge of herbs and their uses as medicine. Among the members of the Midewiwin lying, stealing, and other bad behavior were serious offenses. The Medicine Society was therefore not only for healing, but was the focal point in the Ojibwa's religious life.

According to legend, the god Manabus brought the Midewiwin ceremony to the Indians. Manabus was like an Indian, but he had the power to do things men could not do. For example, he could change himself into an animal whenever he wished, and he could converse with rocks and trees. He was also a great trickster.

The Ojibwa believed that serious illness was caused by supernatural powers. Therefore, to diagnose the trouble and to find a cure the services of a medicine man were necessary.

After having a great illness that required the cure of a medicine man, a person might decide to join the Midewiwin Society. Or his guiding spirit, the dream person, might tell him in a dream to seek membership for his own good.

To become a member of the Society a person had to possess great wealth or have many friends willing to help in sharing the cost. The rituals of initiation were conducted by four old medicine men, and they had to be paid equally for their services.

It was customary for a candidate to enter the lodge of the oldest of these men and, after the proper exchange of formalities, bring forth and display his offerings. If the gifts were valuable enough, and if he had brought four of everything, the medicine man then asked the meaning of the gifts. The candidate told him he wished to become a member of the Medicine Society, whereupon the old man offered to call the other three medicine men together for their consent.

The next morning the elder sent invitation sticks and tobacco to the other men. Accepting the tobacco and returning the invitation sticks indicated their willingness to help.

Once all the medicine men agreed to go ahead, the instruction period started for the candidate. Seated in the rear of the oldest medicine man's wigwam were the four medicine men, with the candidate on their left. In front of them lay the many gifts, and on a white tanned fawn skin stood the sacred *towaka,* the medicine drum.

Its frame was a short section of a basswood log, hollowed out with much labor. It was fitted with a tight bottom made from the same tree. This drum frame held two fingers' depth of water, and stretched over the open end was a dampened, tanned buckskin, held in place with a wooden hoop. The drumstick, one end strikingly carved to represent the beak of the loon, rested across the drumhead. In front of the drum stood a wooden bowl heaped with tobacco, plus four old gourd rattles, their wooden handles shining with age and much use.

A young boy tended the fire, adding to it from time to time bunches of sweet grass and cedar for incense.

Extending his hands over the sacred drum, rattles, and tobacco, the leader prayed, calling on the mythical hero founder of the Medicine Lodge, Manabus, or the Great Manitou, the Sun, and the Thunderbirds. He called upon the good as well as the evil spirits, asking them to appear in spirit and accept the offerings of tobacco.

At the end of the prayer, those in the wigwam responded by saying "Hau," whereafter the three medicine men smoked and listened while the oldest took up the drum.

With the beaked drumstick he gave four sharp strokes on the drum. Then in a solemn tone he began to recite the origin of the Midewiwin, hushing his voice to a whisper whenever he mentioned the Great Powers by name.

At the end of this recital there was a recess for refreshments and relaxation, which lasted the time it took to smoke a pipe. Then one of the other medicine men took over the instructions.

He told the candidate about the powers above and the powers below. He related how in ancient times the members of the lodge had been seated according to the powers of their medicine bags. Any skin, or a part of it, from certain animals could be used as a medicine bag, because each of these animals had given some special power to help man. The animals of the powers were the otter, mink, marten, and weasel. Next came the bear, panther, wolf, and horned owl.

The third instructor sang four songs in honor of each of these animals for the candidate in the medicine lodge. However, as the songs were so many in number, the candidate would purchase them later and learn them at leisure.

Finally the fourth elder took over. From him the candidate learned about certain articles that would be given him ceremonially during the actual initiation.

One of these articles was a tanned otter skin, and it was to become the new member's medicine bag. The nostrils of the bag were stuffed with red-dyed hawk down. The underside of the legs and the tail was covered with fringed pieces of buckskin, dyed blue and decorated with floral designs worked in porcupine quills.

In the medicine bag were several medicines, including sacred blue face paint, the color of the sky, and a mysterious brown powder containing a seed, wrapped together with a fresh-water clamshell.

All of these preparatory instructions could be given at any time during the year, providing four of the leading medicine men were available.

The actual initiation into the Society took place in spring or fall. Those were the times of the year when most of the families came together for a period of visiting, games, gossip, and, of course, the great Midewiwin ceremony. A typical ceremony might have taken place as follows.

Now it was spring again, and in an opening in the forest the Midewigan—the Medicine Lodge—had been erected. It measured a full hundred feet in length, but was only twenty feet wide. The lodge was dome shaped and made from poles, which were covered with bark and rush mats. It was built so that its end openings faced east and west.

Three nights and three days had been spent by the four masters and their pupil. First he was

given a ceremonial sweat bath to purify his body. Then he was given the final instructions. His initiation fee, the four sets of valuable goods—clothing, robes, weapons, and other items—were hung from the ridgepole and dedicated.

As the sun sank low in the sky, the four medicine men and the candidate came into the Midewigan. Following them were the men and women members of the Society.

Various ceremonies were conducted throughout this fourth night. Toward morning the chief medicine man came before the candidate, who stood facing east. From his medicine bag he drew forth his sacred clamshell cup and the powder containing the seed. This he mixed into a drink while he chanted a song to the otter. He then handed the mixture to the young man, who drank it.

Following this ritual another medicine man came forward singing. When his song ended the young man bent over, coughing hard, and in a few moments, as if he had just coughed it up, he held in his hand a small seashell, called the Megis. This shell was the main emblem of the Midewiwin Society, because, according to their own tradition, the original home of the Ojibwa was by the salt waters of the Atlantic.

Holding out his hand, the candidate displayed the Megis to the four winds, all the while chanting a medicine song.

Now the third medicine man stepped up and with the sacred blue paint colored the candidate's face. During this part of the ceremony the medicine man sang four songs.

The fourth and last medicine man finally came to stand before the candidate and the leader. Carrying the otter-skin medicine bag, he too sang four songs, the most famous of which is called "This Medicine Land." Then he placed the medicine bag at the feet of the young man.

The leading medicine man and the candidate now stood up, and the medicine man conducted him around the lodge four times. The fourth time he was led to a seat near the western end of the lodge where he sat down, facing east.

As he sat there the remaining medicine men came toward him from the east end of the lodge. One of them, holding his medicine bag chest-high with both hands, sang a song called "Shooting the New Member." Then he blew on the head of the otter bag and rushed forward as if to attack the candidate. Just short of his target he stopped and, jerking the otter bag upward, he gave a loud war cry. As if he had been struck a blow with the medicine bag, the young man staggered slightly.

The second and third medicine men also made these sham attacks, and each time the young man reeled as if struck.

The attack by the fourth medicine man was so violent that the candidate fell to the ground. As he lay there his last attacker placed the medicine bag across the apparently unconscious young man's back. Thereafter, it would be his.

GRAY·WOLF

At a sign from the leader the other medicine men came forward and raised the new member to his feet, shaking him gently to remove their "shots" and to restore him to life.

Throughout the entire Midewigan, there was rejoicing. A delicious stew, as well as a soup made of bear and turtle meat, of partridge, and of young ducks, was served in steaming earthen kettles. During the feast there was laughter and jesting, and when at last the personal wooden food bowls were scraped clean, the drummers started to beat out a fast dance step.

The people sang four songs before the dance actually started. Then the men and women danced around the lodge, their new brother with them.

By now the sun stood noon high in the sky. The fine ceremonial gifts had been distributed, and all the members filed out through the west door. As they went by the new member they sang, "You, my brother, I pass my hand over you. I thank you."

He had now passed the first degree. If he wished

to go ahead, and could afford it, there were seven more. However, due to the mounting costs of the degrees, most Indians did not go beyond the fourth stage in these medicine rituals.

7 ◈ SHAMANS OF THE TOTEM PEOPLE

LIKE the Indians in other parts of the country, the people of the Northwest Coast sought a personal spiritual helper, and they searched long and hard for one. To please the spirit he hoped to encounter, a man cleansed himself by fasting and by bathing in an icy pool. There he scrubbed away all human odors, either with bunches of nettles or with a brush made from a bundle of short twigs.

Once a spirit had been contacted and was

pleased, it could help a man become a great warrior or gain much wealth. The greatest gift the spirit could give a man, however, was the power to cause or cure illness. A man having those gifts became a shaman, or medicine man. *Shaman* is a Siberian word, used most often among the Indians of this region.

The Northwest Coast Indians had a strict system regarding status in their villages. Ranking highest were, of course, the chief and his family. Then came the nobility, next the commoners, and lastly the slaves.

To reach a high position within the tribe a person had to be a member of one of the two upper classes, except in one instance. If a spirit had bestowed upon the lowest commoner the power to become a shaman, he gained prestige. He became a public figure, and the entire village gathered in the "spirit house" to watch him perform his rites while treating a patient.

Shamans were great sleight-of-hand artists. It

is little wonder that they were either honored or feared, or in some cases a little of both.

Their regalia differed from village to village. Some let their hair grow to its full length, leaving it in a tangled, uncombed state as their badge. Around their neck they wore beautifully carved necklaces, and they carried a carved bone tube with which to blow away sickness and to catch souls.

During the performance of the rites that showed how powerful he was, the shaman had many helpers. These helpers were not, as in other tribes, learning to become medicine men. Rather, they were people in the shaman's direct employ, paid to do his bidding.

The shaman of the Northwest and his "cures" contrast greatly with the Navaho medicine man, for the shaman relied on tricks and sham. The plank house where he performed healing rituals was specially constructed. It had double walls, trap doors, and tunnels. Long, hollow tubes of kelp—a seaweed some species of which reach a length of two hundred feet—were hidden beneath the plank floor. There they acted as speaking tubes for the shaman, enabling him to produce "spirit voices" and make them seem to come from different areas of the room.

The rites were performed after dark, and "flying spirits"—which were really carved figures—could be made to appear and disappear overhead.

A shaman's performance must have been very effective. A central fire in the pit lighted up the audience, but the rest of the large room was in deep darkness. At the same time the people's tall shadows made the room behind them appear even darker. That was just what the shaman wished, as the dark shadows helped to hide the strings on the flying spirits from view.

Standing before the large gathering, the shaman sang and shook his carved rattle while he called upon the spirits to show themselves. As his singing increased in volume, the "spirits" appeared, wearing beautifully carved masks representing men, animals, and birds. From neck to knees they were covered with long strands of shredded cedar bark. They were the shaman's helpers.

Coming from behind the double walls, they appeared to be passing through the walls from outside. Just beyond the firelight, behind the crowd, they danced, the beaks of the bird masks opening and closing with a clattering sound. Human and animal masks opened to reveal other faces beneath, then closed again. The darkness blotted out the fine strings the dancers were pulling to change the masks, and when finally these "spirits" returned to their hiding places, they again seemed to vanish through the plank walls.

Now the shaman called on the spirits whose homes were in the world below. Silently the shaman's helpers under the floor slid away a well-oiled trap door and, slowly walking up a ramp, they appeared to float right out of the floor.

As the shaman called to unseen spirits in a loud

voice, asking them questions, his helpers answered through the hollow kelp tubes. The answers might come from beneath the central fire, from behind the place where the chief was sitting, from somewhere among the rafters—from the carved raven on top of a house post—or from any other unlikely place within the "spirit lodge."

The shamans of the Northwest Coast, who were both men and women, had the power to bring bad luck or sickness. It was said of some of them that they caused illnesses so that they would be paid for performing the cure.

8 ◆ THE MEDICINE MAN OF TODAY

TODAY many Indians have adopted the white man's religion. However, some of the old customs still are followed here and there. The Iroquois Nation in New York State is divided. One group follows the teachings of the Christian Church, while another group follows the teachings of the old Longhouse and Handsome Lake. The members of the Longhouse still believe in the healing rites of the False-face Society.

The Apache Indians, too, follow some of their old customs, and although many of the rituals are no longer in use they are not forgotten. The largest remaining ceremony is the Mountain Spirit Dance. In that ceremony the medicine man is the leader, as he was in years gone by.

Among the Ute Indians the Christian Church never got a strong foothold, and their medicine man is still very much in demand.

The Ojibwa and the Winnebago Indians, especially those living in more remote areas, depend largely on their medicine men. The Ojibwa still follow the Midewiwin ceremony, and the Winnebago perform their Dream Dance. These rituals resemble one another in many respects.

The chapter dealing with the medicine man of the Navaho is as true today as it was centuries ago. One change, however, is the cooperation between their medicine men and the white doctors.

This change was slow in coming, for when a Navaho died his hogan was destroyed, and the place where it had stood was shunned. As was bound to happen, a few Indians did consent to being taken to the white man's hospital, and some of them were so ill that they died. Because the hospital was not destroyed after a patient's death, the Navaho believed that the spirit of the dead man remained within its walls. This superstition kept others from going to the white medicine man.

The medicine man, who wanted always to help his people, did much to bring the Indian and the white doctor together. In some cases the medicine man went with his patient to the hospital. There he saw the patient admitted, talked with the doctor, and assured the Indian that everything would be well. As a last reassuring gesture, he gathered up the patient's clothes and took them away with him.

The Indian now had faith that he would be cured. While the white man worked over him at the hospital, he knew that the medicine man would perform a healing ceremony over his clothes, chanting the old medicine songs and shaking the medicine rattle over them.

Sometimes the doctor gave up, claiming that the patient was incurable. Records show that in some of these cases the medicine man took the patient back home and, by placing him outdoors in the sun, administering daily sweat baths, and giving the patient a proper diet, the medicine man cured the person completely.

More and more Indians have benefited from modern medical science. Yet we cannot overlook the fact that the really sincere medicine man was a healer of both body and mind. He had a vast knowledge of several hundred plants, herbs, and barks, and he knew at what stage in their growth they were at their potent best for medicinal use. He knew many cures, including an inoculation against rabies.

And so the medicine man is still in evidence, especially among the tribes of the Southwest. But he also works among other tribes in which al-

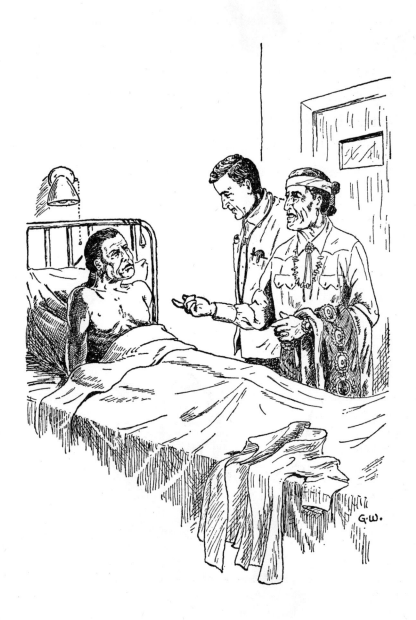

legiance is divided between the white man's church and the medicine man.

When the old culture disappears, the medicine man may disappear too, which will be unfortunate. He worked with his people and for them, keeping them well and secure. Without him the American Indian might not have survived to this day.